MY MASTER'S
Touch

MY MASTER'S
Touch

Lynda M. Nelson

Galleon Publishing

Library of Congress Catalog Card Number:
96-94503
ISBN   0-9645810-0-0

Printed in the United States of America.

10 9 8 7 6 5 4 3 2 1

Galleon Publishing
P.O. Box 50083
Idaho Falls, ID 83401

Illustrations
by Patrick Caldwell

Cover design and production
by Jericho Communication Group

With loving thanks

To my best friend while I was growing up—
who taught me smiles, love, and kindness—
my mother, Betty.

and

To my father, Felix,
whose faith and encouragement
helped make my dreams come true.

Dedication

In loving memory of
John Wendell Gerber,
Father,
Grandfather,
Great-grandfather,
August 6, 1904–September 7, 1996

There is no value great enough to place
on the loving welcome you gave each of us
as we joined your family here on earth.

Day by day, you showed us how to meet life's challenges.
Then you showed us how to endure bravely to the end.

Now, one last time, you've gone ahead
to prepare the way for us.
We send our love and thanks across all time and space,
until we meet again beyond that heavenly veil.

A Rare Friendship

Long ago, in a faraway land, there lived a young boy and his burro. The little boy was fair and kind and greatly loved by his father and mother. The burro was small and gray with a black stripe running down his back and a long, beautiful black tail. His mane was black and the stiff hair stood straight up from his neck, and his belly was white. His two floppy ears were gray and just touched with black at the tips. They seemed to be moving all of the time, those ears—sometimes toward a sound, sometimes back flat or out to the side, or straight up to talk. The little boy could understand so much of what the burro wanted to say just by looking in his big brown eyes and watching his expressive ears.

My name is Meshak and I am that little burro. I called the boy my master. This is my story and I have to tell it now for I am very old and very tired. Soon my master will come and I must follow him once more. But before I go, I want you to know of our life together.

I remember the night my master was born. I opened my eyes as I heard his mother whimpering in pain. I lay warmly snuggled up next to my mother and watched this beautiful woman fight bravely against the pain and fear of childbirth. She smiled encouragingly at her frightened husband while he hovered over her, trying desperately to help. She tried hard to close her lips against the pain, but in the end, I heard her cry out in agony and beg for help. Her husband spoke in hushed tones, trying to encourage and reassure his suffering wife. His hands shook in fear and his eyes darted from side to side, desperate to find someone, something to help. When their tiny son finally appeared, they sobbed together in happiness and relief.

He came into the world as we all do—wet and wrinkled, crying out at the cold night air. His father quickly dried the squalling infant, then bundled him into a warm blanket. Gently, he laid the tiny baby in his wife's tired but eager arms, then snuggled close to both of them. They spoke softly, welcoming him to the world and pouring their love over their newborn son.

Soon, visitors began arriving to congratulate the parents and to welcome the child with gifts. They spoke excitedly of his bright eyes and his strong fingers and cheered his arrival. When the shadow of the last visitor moved through the opening on his way out, the mother and her child finally slept.

———◆———

As soon as he could crawl, I started to see him in my stable from time to time. I still recall the first time he

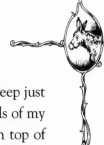

crawled across the straw to where I lay, trying to sleep just a few more minutes. His tiny fists grabbed handfuls of my shaggy coat and soon he was crawling right up on top of my side. It didn't hurt because he was so light. Then he crawled up near my head, laid across my neck, and started trying to grab my ears. I flicked them back and forth so that he couldn't get ahold of them while I watched him out of the corner of my eye. He must have thought it was a wonderful game because he gurgled with happy laughter and patted my face enthusiastically with his little hands. His squeals of joy were a delight to me.

My life, to that point, had been spent by the side of my mother. She had lived long and served her mistress well. But after I was born, she grew weaker and weaker. Then just a few days before, she had nuzzled me with her loving nose for the last time. She died quietly in her sleep. Suddenly, I was all alone. My heart ached for her loving touch and encouraging nickers. Though there were other animals in the small barn, none of them could take her place.

But this little fellow was something new, something delightful. Soon he was crawling all over me, pulling my hair, pinching my nose, twisting my ears, and yanking my tail. For just a moment, he looked right into my eyes. My heart stopped and chills of joy raised the hair up and down my neck as he stared deep into my soul. Then a beautiful smile lit up his face and he laughed. I laughed right back with a soft hee-haw. He sat back and waved his dimpled fists in delight. I held very still, my heart racing as I watched to see what he would do next. I thor-

oughly enjoyed his antics and hoped that he would stay forever. I was utterly enchanted with him.

It wasn't long before I heard his mother frantically calling his name. She dashed into the stable through the big, open gate. I looked up at her as she rushed to my stall, but I didn't move for fear I would hurt the little fellow. The instant relief on her face was easy to read.

"Oh, Meshak, thank you for being so careful." She reached down and picked up the adventurous baby, then patted me on the head. "You're such a good little burro."

As she turned to leave, I scrambled to my feet and trotted after them. But just before I reached the opening, the stable gate shut, leaving me trapped inside. I looked at the gate for a moment, then turned and shuffled back to my stall and flopped down in the straw. She had taken him away and with him, a bit of light went out of the stable. I was alone again.

But I wasn't lonely for long. I would see him from time to time as he grew up. He didn't escape often from his mother's watchful care, but when he did, he would head straight for my stall. His visits always brightened my day. The next time he came to see me, I was standing up eating my dinner of hay and oats after a long and tiring day spent learning to pull a small cart for this baby's father. The adventurous little fellow came crawling through the stable gate, heading straight for my stall. I was surprised to see him, but very pleased also. I held really still, waiting to see what he would do.

When he finally crawled into my stall, he stopped, then sat back on his bottom and waved his tiny fists at

me. With that enchanting smile on his round little face, he laughed and talked a bunch of gibberish which I didn't understand. Then he rolled over onto all fours and crawled right under my belly. I really had to bend my neck around to keep looking at him. He grabbed ahold of my right front leg first with one hand, then grabbed a fist full of hair with the other and began to pull himself up next to my leg. Soon, he was standing there, gently swaying back and forth on his tiny feet, but holding on with amazing strength. His giggle was infectious. I laughed back at him with some soft hee-haw noises.

He seemed to think that was really funny for he giggled delightedly. Next, he started walking around me on his wobbly legs, grabbing different pieces of my shaggy coat for support as he worked his way from one end to the other. He seemed to think he really had something special when he found my tail, because he flapped it up and down and pulled hard. When he got ahold of the long hair with both hands, he just fell right over into the straw, for it was flimsy and didn't support him.

As he struggled unsuccessfully to turn over onto his stomach in the deep straw, I turned around, being very careful not to step on him, so that I was facing him again. Curiously, I reached my nose down to sniff at him and take a closer look. He thought that was very entertaining too, for he began to giggle. Reaching up with both hands, he grabbed ahold of the hair on the sides of my face and pulled himself up into a sitting position. There we were, eye to eye, nose to nose. Once again, he stared straight into my eyes, into my soul, as though with a

bright, searching light. My heart raced and I held my breath as a delicious warmth spread outward from my heart clear to the bottom of each hoof.

The moment passed and suddenly he tried to take a bite of the softest part of my nose. I just couldn't stand there and let him do that, so I shook my head—just a little bit. From behind me, I heard the gentle laughter of his beautiful mother. The baby still hadn't let go of my face, so I couldn't turn my head to look at her. With my head hanging down, held tightly by those two determined little hands, all I could do was turn my eyes and ears sideways and silently plead for her help.

"Oh, my adventurous little son, let go of Meshak." Her gentle hands reached down and loosened his grip on my cheeks, then she picked her son up and settled him on her hip. I was delighted when her hand brushed down my neck and scratched behind my ears. I loved his mother too, because she was always tender and kind.

"Meshak, thank you for being so gentle and patient with him." I watched expectantly as she walked over to the oat box and scooped out a cup full of those delicious grains. I pricked up my ears and let out a very soft "hee-haw" when she poured them into my food trough.

"Here, you deserve a treat for being such a good little burro." I munched on the grain as she closed the gate behind them and they were gone.

———◆———

As my little master grew and learned to walk, he visited me more often. Before long, he was pulling himself

up onto my back.

"Meshak, hold still. Here I come!" My master made a running start, then threw himself onto my back as high as he could reach. He grabbed fistsful of my hair and hung on tight.

"Almost there, now . . . don't! move!" he grunted. Kicking, pulling, and wiggling, he finally pulled himself up until he was high enough to throw his right leg over my back.

"Almost . . . there . . ." Then, whump!!! Neither of us knew what happened, but the next moment he not only pulled himself up onto my back, but somehow kept right on going and fell off the other side into the deep straw.

He lay in the straw and looked up at me as I brayed out my laughter, "Hee-haw, hee-haw!"

"You moved!" he accused me, then he jumped up, dusted himself off and tried again.

Once my master learned how to stay on, he was urging me to run through the meandering streets of our little village. I didn't run or even walk very fast for a long time. He was eager and fearless, but I was afraid he would fall off.

"Meshak, you're a stubborn old burro!" He laughed in frustration.

I wobbled my ears back at him and silently called him impetuous. When he rode on my back I was responsible for his safety and I took that responsibility seriously, no matter how much he pleaded for more speed.

The River

The years passed and my master grew to be a good rider. We galloped over the hills around our village, the warm wind blowing through our hair. We collected firewood, went to the market, and watched the farmers in the fields and the vineyards. It was my lot in life to carry heavy, often cumbersome burdens. But they were burdens of his making and somehow that made them easier to bear.

We went to the river one day just to play. There was a large group of children from the village splashing and playing in the shallow water. It was a hot afternoon, so my master urged me to walk straight into the river where he purposely fell off sideways into the water. He came up spluttering and laughing, wiping the cool water from his eyes.

"Meshak, that was really fun! I'm going to do it again." He climbed right back on and fell off again. The next time, he worked hard to stand on my rump. He stood very straight, arms extended out from his sides,

then slowly tipped backwards until he fell off into the water. This was new and strange, but also fun. So I patiently stood very still while he perfected this new form of entertainment. The other boys were soon scrambling through the water to climb on my back and fall off.

My master glanced toward the riverbank, then called to the other boys to stop splashing for a moment. "Wait, I see a new friend who wants to come play with us." Everyone turned to see where my master pointed.

There, sitting in the grass beside the bright water sat a little boy with twisted legs. His eyes burned with the desire to play in the water with all of the other boys, but his crippled legs made such fun impossible.

My master turned to look deep into my eyes. "Meshak, shall we invite him to play with us?" I twitched my ears in response.

"He can't play out here! He'll drown!" an older boy named Jacob scoffed.

"I'm sure that with our help, he will be able to stay on Meshak's back." My master spoke quietly and smiled into Jacob's eyes. "He won't drown. But he *will* get very wet and have a wonderful time."

Jacob stared into my master's eyes for a moment, then a crooked smile brightened his face. "We'll all help . . . get him wet, and keep him from drowning."

All of the boys had been listening intently, but now they cheered and smiled eagerly as I followed my master. We splashed through the water to the riverbank and he sat down beside the crippled boy.

"What's your name?" he asked.

"Joshua." The little boy spoke to my master, but his dark brown eyes darted from me to the boys in the river, then up into my master's eyes.

"We need another boy on our team. Would you like to come out and get wet with the rest of us?"

The boy hesitated. "You don't need me." His eyes lowered to his twisted legs. Bitterness edged his voice as he spoke. "I can't walk into the water, and I can't swim either." He started to scoot away, walking with his hands and dragging his useless legs.

"Wait!" My master reached out and touched his slender arm. The boy looked up into my master's eyes once more.

"You don't have to swim or even walk." He pointed to me. "See? I have a wonderful friend named Meshak. He wants to carry you out where you can splash in the water with the rest of us."

Joshua looked at me. That was my cue and I bobbed my head up and down.

The sadness left his eyes, replaced by a sparkling light of excitement. A joke, a smile, and soon Joshua was laughing at different things my master said. Scooping him up with both arms, my master lifted Joshua up onto my back. While he clutched my mane tightly with both hands, his legs dangled loosely on either side of my back. Together, the three of us moved out to deep water. Joshua clung desperately to my mane, fearful and happy at the same time. I walked carefully so that he would not fall off, and my master supported him with one hand as he walked by my side.

Suddenly, water erupted on all sides and Joshua was immediately in the center of a massive water fight, laughing and shouting with the other boys. Holding tight to my mane with one hand, he bravely reached the other hand down to where the river water touched his knees and eagerly splashed back as hard as he could.

Just as I felt Joshua's hands grow weaker and knew that his strength was spent, my master was there at our side, a supporting arm around the boy. Joshua's new friends waved and shouted good-bye as we took him back to the riverbank.

Joshua's older sister had come to find him and stayed to watch the scene in the river. I saw that her eyes were full of tears. My master lifted the boy from my back and placed him in his sister's arms.

"Th-thank you!" she hesitated, "I can't tell you how much this means for my brother to be able to play with the other boys." She turned to carry him home, then spoke back over her shoulder. "Bless you—both."

As she walked away, Joshua looked back past her shoulder and enthusiastically waved one arm while shouting his thanks.

We raced back into the water and once again my master climbed up onto my back to stand up and tip over backwards into the water. Soon, all the boys were following his example, climbing up on my back and falling off backwards. It wasn't long before three of them were sitting on my back and more were trying to scramble on as well. I decided that was enough, so I just sat down in the water and they all slid off backwards. Laughter and

giggles erupted along with splashing water. Then they were dousing me and themselves.

I stood back up and shook the water from my shaggy coat. I blasted the air with my loudest "hee-haw" and shocked them all. Amid delighted laughter, they mobbed me, seven or eight boys trying to scramble up onto my back at the same time. I waited until they were so heavy I could hardly stand, then I just laid right down in the river and dumped them all. "Kersplash!!!"

Spluttering and laughing at the same time, they all let go of me and swam away. I was so pleased with myself that I rolled over onto my back and kicked my legs high up in the air. Water went down my nose, making me cough and sneeze. I thrashed around in the water desperately until I finally struggled to my feet, snorting, bucking, and spraying water all over everyone.

That day will remain with me forever as a sparkling memory of fun and laughter. But, more importantly, I knew that my master had taken his place as the leader of the boys who played with him in the river. I watched them be drawn to him by his gentle laughter and the light that shone in his eyes. Then, with only a few words being spoken, he taught them, by example, the joy of compassion and service. It was a lesson I would watch him teach many times in the years to come.

Out of the Dark

I felt older and wiser than my master while he was young, but somewhere in his eighth year, I began to notice changes in him. He seemed to grow wiser, and though he still laughed and played like other young boys, I noticed differences. Slowly and subtly, he truly became the leader and I took my place as the follower. Our days and times of simple joys were passing quickly.

When his parents decided he was old enough, my master began waking me up before dawn and we would go up into the hills around our village to gather wood for his mother's cooking fire.

Early one particular morning, I was peacefully sleeping, dreaming of frolicking and playing in the river, when the stable gate rattled against the wood and leather hinges. I reluctantly opened my eyes and watched as it slowly swung open and a dim light appeared in the opening. Several of the chickens roosting high in the rafters ruffled their feathers out a bit more and settled back into

sleep. The big rooster, perched on the highest rafter in the barn, opened a sleepy eye and peered at the intruder warily. His red and brown feathers flattened closer to his body as he prepared for possible battle. My master stepped through the gate, holding a rust-colored clay oil lamp high above his head by the small handle at one end. The tiny flame formed a pool of warm light around my master, casting the far corners of the barn into deep shadows. The old cock relaxed again, closed his little red eyes, and fluffed his feathers back up before returning to sleep.

A whisper of cold night air crept into the barn, causing the two milk goats, the sheep, and her lamb to shift in their sleep and lazily lift heavy eyelids.

"Go back to sleep, everyone. I have come to take Meshak up into the hills and the sun will not be up for a long time yet." My master spoke gently to each of the animals as he quietly crept past their stalls.

"Good morning, Meshak." When he reached the tiny space at the end of the barn where I slept, I was already standing and shaking the warm, fragrant straw from my shaggy coat. "It looks like you wanted to sleep a little bit longer." He brushed the remaining straw from my back.

I reached out to touch him with my nose and nickered a soft welcome. I hungered for that tingly chill and delightful warmth which spread through my body whenever he touched me or looked into my eyes. I had begun to live for my master's touch.

My long ears flopped from side to side as I shook my head back and forth. The shaking continued on down my short neck, across my striped back, and ended with a vigorous hind-quarters and tail shake. Ooh, that felt marvelous! One giant, toothy yawn and I was thoroughly awake. I let out a soft braying sound and pushed gently against his chest with my forehead, hoping he would give me some of those delicious oats.

"You seem to want something, Meshak. Now what could it possibly be, my friend?" He smiled as I pushed my muzzle into his empty hand and nickered softly while looking up, pleading with my eyes. He chuckled, then set the lamp carefully on a small shelf built into a support post.

"My fuzzy friend, I'm so glad you go out with me on these dark mornings. You make all of my chores seem more like fun than work." My master spoke to me in low tones as he took a moment to scratch behind my floppy ears and down the front of my little gray face, just to the black ring of hair around my nose. He knew I loved to be scratched in all those places that I couldn't reach for myself.

"I know what you really want. It's those oats! I think you love me most for the oats I feed you." I nodded my head up and down and my mouth watered in eager anticipation when he reached into the wooden bin and offered me oats from his cupped hands.

As I happily munched on the grain, he filled a small sack with oats. He turned to me with one more small handful and let me slurp them right out of his cupped fingers. While I chewed contentedly, he twisted the little bag closed and placed it inside one of the pack bags

that he fastened across my back. Careful not to tip the small lamp and spill the oil, he lifted it back down from the wooden shelf.

"I'm ready, Meshak. Let's go." As he held it out in front to light our path, my master led the way through the gate, then turned to close it. Once again on our way, the small lamp continued to cast its welcome light only steps in front of our quiet feet.

"The sky is very dark tonight, Meshak. I can't see any stars." I nickered in response and shivered just a bit.

"Yes, it's cold out here too, this morning." He stayed just in front of me as we walked between the high walls of the closely packed houses. Light reflected from my master's lamp and cast lonely, eery shadows all around us. We had been out in the early morning darkness before, but today seemed different—darker, lonelier.

We were just a few turnings away from the small city gate when the little oil lamp grew dim. It flickered a moment—then went out. Instantly, we were plunged into blinding darkness.

"Oh, no!" Both of us stumbled to a halt. I waited for him to rekindle the lamp as my eyes widened, searching for any tiny bits of light. I could smell and hear the sounds of the sleeping city around me, but I was still nervous about being in the dark. He shook the lamp back and forth, but I did not hear the friendly slosh of oil in its little chamber. A chilling tingle went down my neck and back as the cold breeze tugged at my mane and tail like some unseen ghost in the night.

"Meshak," I felt my master's hand grip my mane

tightly. "It's so dark! I can't see anything." He moved closer to me. We huddled together in the darkness, hearing and feeling a sudden gust of wind whistle through the streets, whipping bits of sand and dust viciously past our ankles. My master wrapped his arms around my neck and buried his face in the side of my neck while I closed my eyes, tucked my tail and dropped my ears to protect them from the blowing grit.

Just as suddenly as it had attacked, the wind died away to a gentle, cool breeze once again. I opened my eyes and flapped my ears back and forth, listening again for sounds in the darkness.

"Whew! That was scary." My master stood up straight once more and loosened his grip on my mane.

"Meshak, my friend, I made a big mistake. I forgot to fill the lamp with oil before I left home." I could hear a little bit of worry and fear—and wonder—in his voice. I leaned closer to my master and felt his small body quiver. I was shocked to realize that I had forgotten how small he really was. His wisdom and confidence made him seem older. But here in the dark, as we shared the warmth of being together and the fear of traveling in the black night alone, I realized that he was still just a young boy—and he needed me.

"It feels a lot colder out here without the light," he whispered. I nickered in agreement. The walls of the houses seemed to hang over us, seemed to move in and trap us. My master had been leading the way before, but now he clung to my shaggy hair as he felt his way through the darkness till he was at my side. I held very still while he scrambled up onto my back.

Leaning forward, he whispered in my ear, "Meshak, you see so much better in the dark than I do. I know you can find the gate even without the light. Be my eyes this morning, my friend and guide me once more."

A thoughtful tone came into his voice as he continued. "I will always remember how lonely the dark is when the warmth and light of the lamp are gone. Help me now and I promise never to forget to fill my lamp again."

Then his little fists clutched my mane tightly and a new thrill ran up my neck and made my ears twitch. I slowly started walking down the street, feeling very brave and important. My master had faith in me. He needed me and I would not fail him. My heart seemed to swell with happiness and pride. I felt I could do anything through the touch of my master's hand.

The street between the high walls was almost pitch black. "Ooh, it's eery in the city streets when it's dark, Meshak." I felt a chill run through my master's body as the clip clop of my hooves echoed off the walls. I twitched my ears back and forth, listening carefully and watching the shadows for danger.

"Just a few steps further, Meshak." My master's voice was calm and reassuring. "I know we're almost there. Another corner and we should see the lamp from the gate." His gentle hands patted my neck in encouragement, his legs warm where they held tightly to my sides.

Through the dark, all the noises seemed louder, closer at hand. A loud, scratchy, scurrying sound signaled the

passage of a creature in the night. The distant screech of two fighting cats sent shivers up my spine and my master held on tighter. I moved a little faster.

Suddenly, we heard footsteps pounding toward us. My master sucked in a frightened breath when a huge figure raced around the corner just ahead, rushing toward us in the darkness. We could barely make out his robed and masked shape, a dark cape flapping wildly in his wake. I jumped to the side of the street, my master clinging desperately to my mane, his legs tight around my belly.

The man carried no light as he dashed past us without even glancing in our direction. The sound of his running steps faded quickly behind us and once more we were alone. My heart was thudding in my chest and I broke out in a cold sweat of fear and relief. My master wrapped his shaking arms around my neck and clung to me, dragging painful breaths into his lungs. I shook my head and snorted hot air from my nostrils, then slowly started walking again. Soon I was breathing easier and my master relaxed.

He sat back up and spoke to me again. "Oh, thank you, Meshak! If you hadn't moved over, he would have run right over us!" He sounded relieved as he patted my neck.

Gradually, in the dust before us, we could just barely make out a soft glimmer of light, only slightly lighter than the blackness around us.

"I think I can see some light, Meshak." I bobbed my head up and down as I walked a little faster. Clip clop, clip clop. The light grew a little brighter.

"It seems such a long way in the dark, Meshak. It never feels this far when we have light and can see our way." He was still whispering, still afraid of the dark.

When at last we came to the next intersection in the winding streets and turned the corner, our path was lit once more. A single lamp glowed in the distance, beckoning us to come into its light and warmth. Our pathway grew brighter until finally we stood before the glowing lamp at the gate.

"Look back, Meshak. The darkness behind us seems even scarier now that we have finally come into the light." I glanced back into the darkness then turned to look into his eyes. "But now I feel safe and warm again, Meshak." The lantern cast its golden glow all around us now and I too felt safe and warm. It was very much like the feeling I experienced each time my master came to get me from the stable. In his presence, I felt security, safety, and love.

"Oh, Meshak, I knew you could do it. Thank you, thank you!" My master patted my neck enthusiastically and gave me one more big hug. I was so proud and pleased at his praise that I held my head up as high as I could and swished my tail from side to side.

We rested safely in the glow of the lantern while a cool breeze pushed the clouds across the sky. I watched curiously when my master dropped to his knees and bowed his head for a time. When he stood once again, I looked at him, asking a question with my eyes.

"I was praying, Meshak. Giving thanks to my Father in Heaven for bringing us safely through the dark streets."

I did not understand. I thought I had brought us out of the dark streets. Had someone else been there? This 'Father' my master spoke of? I shook my head in confusion and my master chuckled.

"Meshak, it's all right. One day you'll understand." He smiled into my eyes as he scratched behind my ears. At his touch, I felt that wonderful tingling sensation and the delightful warmth spread through my body once again. My eyelids closed contentedly.

"You deserve a reward, Meshak," my master announced as he poured a handful of oats for me. My eyes popped wide open again. While I munched on oats, my master nibbled on a few of the dates he had brought for himself. We enjoyed a small celebration right there by the city gate in the glow from the street lamp.

It wasn't long before the clouds parted and a late crescent moon cast its silvery glow across the earth, bringing with it more than enough light to brighten our path. We could see where to go once again, so we passed out through the gate and climbed up the road that led into the hills. As the dark clouds drifted further away, a few sparkling stars came out to join the moon in the last moments before dawn.

We paused at the crest of a rise in the road. The dark hills rose in front of us, the shadowy city, a few lights only now beginning to flicker, in the valley behind. Together we raised our eyes to stare at the brightest star in the sky. This was the first of what would be many times when we would stop and stare at that particular star where it glittered so brightly against the dark sky.

We gazed in wonder at the beauty of the starlit heavens, then went on our way. My master hummed a sweet song, keeping beat with the clip clop of my hooves. And I was content.

I carried my master up into the hills until we reached a grove where olive trees grew and old gnarled branches littered the ground. I nibbled the grass at my feet as the moon and stars faded into a new dawn. The rising sun cast its brilliant rays into the early morning sky while my master gathered dead, fallen branches of the trees and piled them neatly in stacks. Once, he stopped to rest and to feed me a handful of oats. I gratefully nuzzled all of them carefully from his small hand.

"Meshak, I've been thinking about the lamp." I perked up my ears and watched my master closely.

"I don't understand it fully yet, but we learned a lesson when the lamp went out this morning." I waited eagerly to see what he would say next, but he finally just shook his head in frustration.

"It's something very important. I can feel it, Meshak," he doubled his fist and tapped his chest twice, "right here." He looked down at his feet, then shook his head. "But I don't know what it is yet." He raised his eyes and gazed straight into mine. I felt my heart almost stop at the power I felt crossing from his eyes to mine.

"You don't know either, do you, my friend?" He looked away and I started breathing again. "I guess I'll just have to wait until I can speak of this with Mother when we get back home."

Standing once more, he gathered together the bun-

dles of branches and tied them carefully into three piles with long leather ropes.

The entire golden ball of the sun had risen above the edge of the earth and its brilliant light illuminated a new day when my master tied one bundle on each side of my back. He tied the final bundle on top of the first two and we were ready to go. The pair of us headed back down the mountainside to the small house where his mother waited for the firewood.

Of Oil and Lamps

*M*other! We're back. Meshak and I have brought enough wood for several days." My master untied one of the bundles and carried it through the open door of his home. I waited patiently by the doorway, twitching the early morning flies away with my tail.

"Thank you. I just put my last piece of wood into the fire," said his mother. "You are in good time!" She leaned down and planted a gentle kiss on top of his head. Standing back up, she looked down at her beloved son and noticed a different expression on his face.

"How was your journey into the hills this morning? Did something happen?" His mother asked. "You look very thoughtful."

I leaned my head through the door, flicking my ears forward to listen while I patiently waited for my master to come unload the remaining firewood from my back.

"We were almost to the city gate when my lamp ran out of oil, Mother. It was very dark and I was frightened.

For a moment I felt totally alone." Then he shared with her all of the events of our morning.

"I'm so sorry your lamp ran out of oil." Her voice echoed her concern. "I can easily understand why you were afraid and felt so lonely."

"It was even more than lonely, Mother. The closest way I can explain it is that I felt—empty—even though Meshak was there, even though I knew my way home."

As his mother and I watched, my master walked across the room to my side and pulled the small lamp from one of my pack bags. He stood beside me and held the lamp with both hands. He turned it from side to side, studying it's simple design as though for the first time. The handle, at one end of the lamp, curved outward in an arch and then back in to provide a comfortable grip. The rounded belly in the center of the lamp was fashioned to hold enough oil to burn for many hours. The opposite end from the handle was shaped in a short, stubby spout. The wick lay inside the spout, one end in the belly of the lamp, the other at the opening of the spout. This way, the wick could syphon the oil up from the belly of the lamp to feed the flame. Purposefully, my master set the empty lamp on the table. Then he walked to a storage shelf and lifted down a large, decorated earthen jar. He carefully pried the lid off, then slowly and cautiously poured oil from the large jar into the smaller reservoir of the lamp.

"Meshak easily found his way through the dark streets and we were safe, Mother. But I can't describe the sensation I felt when we walked into the light of the lantern

by the gate. It made me feel warm and safe. It was a secure feeling—but much—so much more than that." He set the large jar back on the shelf, then turned and picked up the small lamp once more.

His fingers caressed the side of the clay lamp while he continued speaking. "I thought about it all morning while I worked in the hills and as we walked home. I believe there is a special message for me here," my master said. "I just haven't figured it all out yet."

As though performing a ritual, my master held a long taper into his mother's cooking fire until the end was alight. Then he moved it carefully to the wick of the lamp which had been so dark just a few hours ago. As though by magic, however, this time the wick took the flame and a bright light blossomed. With a little puff of air, he blew out the taper and laid it aside. Once again, he lifted the lamp up and looked at it very carefully.

"The lamp is just a simple piece of earthen pottery." He spoke slowly and thoughtfully. "Nothing special. Nothing remarkable. Until I put oil in it and then light that oil." My master held the lamp up at eye level as he studied the bright flame.

"The lamp waits for the light. But without the oil, no light can stay with the lamp. The lamp must be prepared for the light." He was silent for just a moment. "And when it is prepared—with oil—it can hold the flame. Only then can it share its light to help brighten the world." A sweet smile played around his lips as he finished speaking.

"You have learned a very important lesson, my son—

if you truly remember to always keep oil in your lamp." After she spoke, my master's mother took a moment to collect her thoughts while she placed new sticks into her cooking fire. Turning again, she reached for his hand and drew him with her as she sat down at the skillfully crafted wooden table.

"Come—sit with me a moment." She patted the chair beside hers and my master sat down, listening carefully to his mother's words.

"In your life there will come days of darkness, even more dark and frightening than the morning through which you just traveled. You must always keep oil in the lamp inside your heart—here," she gently touched the center of his chest with the palm of her hand, "to help light your way through those dark moments of life."

A tender, knowing smile lifted the corners of her mouth. "Always remember that just as first the moon came up to light your way into the hills, and then the sun rose to light your pathway home, a greater light will come to banish the darkness from your soul." She brushed a lock of hair back from his brow. "If you have faith. If you wait. If you keep your lamp full of oil."

She looked deep into his innocent, inquiring eyes and a small tear ran down her cheek. "There will come dark days in your life, my beloved one. Remember to fill your outside lamp. But more importantly, always fill your inside lamp with the right kind of oil each day before you venture out into the darkness."

She took the lamp from his hands and set it down on the table. "If you do this, you will never lose your

way—and you will brighten the world around you for others." Wrapping her arms around him, she enfolded my master in her loving embrace.

"Mother, that's the key I've been missing." His young voice was eager and excited. "It's not the oil in the lamp that's important, but the oil in our spirit—in our heart—inside us somehow." He wrapped his arms around his mother's neck and gave her a giant squeeze.

"If our inside lamp is empty, we are empty. If we are empty, we can't help ourselves or anyone else." He sat back and looked gravely into his mother's eyes. "I believe that I understand. And yet . . . deep inside . . . I also know that there is much more here that I have yet to discover."

"Never mind for now, my son. When the time comes, you will find your answers." She let him go and stood up again, brushing the tears from her cheeks, a proud, yet poignant smile brightening her face.

"One day you will understand far more than I. But, for here and now, I believe you have learned much."

"Thank you, Mother." He watched her turn back to finish her preparations for their morning meal, pondering her words and looking once more at the bright flame rising from the stubby spout of the oil lamp.

"Please go feed the animals, now, and milk the goats. Then tell your father it is time to eat." She spoke without turning.

My master gently blew out the flame and replaced the smoking lamp on its shelf. His brow was still furrowed in thought as he walked back to the door where I was

intently listening.

I am a simple creature and I did not understand all that was said, but I understood very well the light that shined in my master's eyes each time he looked into my heart. If that was the light from the inside lamp they had talked about, then I did not ever want my master to let his lamp run out of oil. For if his lamp ran dry, my world would be dark indeed.

My back felt lighter and very itchy when my master untied the last two bundles of sticks and pulled them from my back. He placed them in the woodbox standing beside his mother's cooking hearth. Grabbing up the empty milk urn, he came back outside into the sunshine. Together, we walked the few short steps to the stable gate.

He opened the gate wide, letting the bright sunshine and fresh morning air into the warm, musty stable. The sheep and goats were wide awake now, all of them wanting food, the goats bleating to be milked. I hurried to my corner of the small barn and munched hungrily on the new hay my master put in my manger, took a long drink of the cool water he poured for me, then I lay down and rolled ecstatically onto my back. Wiggling back and forth, I worked hard to scratch all those places that itched. I couldn't resist letting the other animals know how I felt, so I exploded the morning air with hee-haws of delight. That made my master laugh and all of the animals turn their eyes to stare.

My master threw new hay to the rest of the animals. A few short minutes later, white streams of milk were

steadily filling the urn and the animals were munching contentedly. As I listened to the squirt, squirt of the milk filling the urn beneath the goat, I saw my master look down at the spot on his chest where his mother's hand had lain and knew that he thought about her words. Then the milking was finished and he picked up the urn. I heard him walk across the narrow street and enter his father's woodshop.

"Mother sent me to bring you home for breakfast, Father." His voice was faint and far away.

"Good. I'm starving!" I recognized the deeper sound of his father's voice. I knew when the two of them walked out into the sunshine, when the father lifted his son, milk and all, and set him high up on his shoulders so that my master could view the world from a higher perch. Then I snuggled into the clean straw and contentedly settled in for a nap as they went home.

I knew my master would come for me again and again and again. And he did. I carried him wherever we went until the day came that his legs were longer than mine. Then I followed him, carrying whatever things he chose to put on my back. It was an honor—*my* honor—to be his beast of burden.

A Path of Stones

The years passed and my master grew to manhood. I too grew older, far beyond the normal age of others of my kind. The black ring around my nose became flecked with gray and it took me longer to get up from my bed of straw each morning. Then, I heard him come, early one morning before the birds were even awake. He carried the little terra cotta lamp and its light fell gently over me as I felt his hand stroke my neck. "Come, old friend, I wish to see the sun rise above the city today."

Obediently, I stumbled to my feet and shook my head to help myself wake up. I nuzzled him in greeting, searching for the oats I liked so much. My master put an old blanket across my back and chuckled, "Here, this should help keep you warm, Meshak— though as old as you are, I should probably call you Methuselah." My master touched me once more and I felt almost young again.

Together we walked down the dark, dusty street until we reached the gate in the city wall, safely walking in the

circle of light cast by the little oil lamp. Quietly, we passed the houses, then the gate, and began our climb up into the foothills. The sky was brilliant with a vast carpet of glittering stars. We crested that same hill where we always stopped and saw again the one star which stood out more brightly than the others, its tail dipping toward the earth in the early hours before dawn. We waited several moments longer than usual as my master raised his eyes to the sparkling star. I, too, lifted my eyes and watched it twinkle and shine as it radiated light onto a dark world.

My master spoke no words as he led the way to our favorite spot at the edge of the grove of olive trees. He sat down upon a rock, still chilly from early morning, while I moved to stand behind him, leaning my head over his shoulder. He blew out the lamp. Together, we gazed down across the silent city and watched the stars disappear and the dark sky slowly lighten. Feathery banks of clouds reflected the golden light that steadily filled the sky, outlining the myriad houses and buildings below us. The indigo sky revolved to iridescent orange and pink, rays of yellow and gold touching the edges of the rocks and trees beside us so that we could see and feel the vibrant colors of the new day.

Small bushes and graceful trees rose around us, interspersed with clumps of straight, stiff grass glistening with sparkling drops of dew. Small birds chirped and twittered in the trees, welcoming the new day. I slowly closed my eyes, contentedly, and hung my head just a bit, trying to stand there and go back to sleep even as the glorious

morning unfolded all around me.

Then my master spoke and I perked up my ears. "Meshak, it is time for me to go. My Father has business to which I must attend—and the time has come. I can wait no longer."

He turned to me and by now my eyes were wide and I was looking right at him, concerned with the strange tone in his voice.

"You need not go with me, old friend." He reached out and stroked my neck, then scratched behind my ears. "I know that the road I must travel will be difficult and even perilous at times. You need not follow me any longer."

Then he took my chin in his hand and looked into my eyes. My heart pounded in my chest and a chilling tingle raised the hair on the back of my neck. The light shining from his eyes burned gently through my own, searching deep inside my heart.

He knew the answer even before he asked the question. "Would you rather stay in the warm stable, my friend? Or will you follow me once again, as you have always done, and share this new road ahead?"

This was no choice. I would go anywhere with my master, live in any conditions. He could read in my eyes my earnest plea that he not leave me behind. His lips turned up in a gentle smile of understanding.

"Thus it has been written—now it shall be done. Let us go tell my mother." He spoke softly, but did not rise. Instead, he continued to stroke my forehead in gentle scratching motions, though his mind was no longer with me.

"She will be sad, I know." His eyes were sad but determined as they gazed out toward the city once more. "But she . . . more than anyone . . . knows how important is my Father's business."

Slowly, my master rose to his feet, his back straight and strong, his head held high. His robes seemed to glow in the early morning light and the golden radiance of the sunrise reflected from his face. It was truly a beautiful morning to start an adventure. Together, we walked down the hill as the sun climbed higher into a glorious sky now turning bright blue.

From that day on, we traveled. It seemed that my master was always searching, always seeking something unknown to me. He talked about his Father and the things his Father wanted him to do. In quiet moments, he often knelt and spoke with his Father. I watched and waited, but I never saw or heard his Father answer him.

I'm only a burro and did not understand many of the things my master tried to explain to me. I struggled to comprehend some of the things he taught to those we met on our travels. But I knew what he meant when he spoke of love and kindness, faith and obedience. And I knew what it meant to follow him. So I followed.

Refining Flame

A dusty haze rose into the hot, early morning air as my master and I climbed high into a desert mountain, far from the shade of the cooling trees. The only vegetation on this barren piece of earth were tufts of sparse grasses, brittle from the baking sunshine. No man cared for this bit of desert, no man toiled to bring it water and watch it blossom. It was left hard, covered with rocks and sand where only lizards, snakes, and scorpions could make a home. It was here that my master came to find the full meaning of the little oil lamp.

My ears and tail were drooping from the heat, my nostrils filled with the dust rising each time my master's feet touched the barren soil. I walked behind my master, my head near the cloth of his robe, watching his cracked and dusty feet. I noticed that the soles were just about worn through on his old, leather sandals. He stumbled a bit as one of his toes struck a rock. But he caught himself and continued walking on and on through this desolate wilderness until he reached a group of large boulders which stood alone in all the heat. My master stopped and turned around so quickly that I bumped right into him before I could stop. I shuffled backwards as quickly as I could, looking up at him with an apology in my eyes.

His understanding hand reached down and patted my side, raising small clouds of dust as he spoke. "Meshak, we will stay here for a time."

I looked around at the arid landscape, wondering what purpose he could have in this barren place. Then I looked back up to my master's eyes.

"I know you don't understand," he smiled gently, "just trust me." Then he pulled the pack bags from my back and set them on the dusty earth beside a rock. He took out the water bag and gave me a sip of water, followed by a mouthful of oats and a handful of the hay which I had been carrying. When he took no food or water for himself, I waggled my ears and looked at him questioningly.

"Don't worry about me, my friend," he answered the unspoken question in my eyes, "I have come here not to feed my body, but to feed my soul."

Many days passed while my master and I stayed in that dry, dusty place. Each day he fed me a meager ration of food and water, but still took none for himself. On the morning of the tenth day, I walked to where he sat, off by himself, and nudged him with my nose. When he turned toward me, I looked into his eyes, silently asking how much longer we would stay here.

His voice was hoarse as he spoke through dry, cracked lips. "Meshak, my faithful friend, I am learning more each day, but I am not yet ready to go."

"I came here to search out the full of meaning in the lesson I learned that dark night when my lamp ran dry." He scratched my dusty ears and stroked my forehead as he gazed into my eyes. "Surely you remember that night?"

I nodded my head as I looked deeper into his eyes, seeking to understand the words he spoke. I was sad to see that his eyes were sunken and red from the blowing dust and blazing sunshine. But the familiar light in his eyes that I loved so well had grown brighter with each passing day. I flicked my ears back and forth to tell him that though I did not fully understand, I trusted him and would wait until he was ready to leave.

More days passed. Each day my master gave me tiny sips of water to drink. Soon I had eaten all of the hay we brought with us, so I nibbled at whatever bits of dried grasses I could find. But my shrunken belly cried out for food and my mouth was dry and swollen, desperate for a quenching pool of water. The sun's heat beat down on me each day, sapping my energy until all I could do was sprawl miserably in the bits of shade cast by the giant rocks. And all the while my master knelt and prayed, pleading with his Father for strength and wisdom, understanding and guidance.

My master suffered far more than I did. But in some way that I did not understand, in his suffering he grew stronger until the day finally came that he stood tall and straight and said it was time to leave.

When we came down from that dry, desolate place, my master had found the answers which he sought and

the bright light that shone from his face told me that his inside lamp was overflowing with oil and would never run dry.

From then on, every morning I awoke to hear my master say, "Meshak, come, follow me." And, happily—even eagerly, I obeyed. I followed him along the seashore and watched the fishermen casting their nets. I followed him through crowds and there were times when I carried bruises left by rocks evil men threw at us. I followed him into the darkness where oftentimes we slept outside under the stars as they flashed brilliantly in the night sky, our only light the clay lamp he had brought from home.

Sometimes we slept under a roof with friends or relatives. But mostly, I followed him to the homes of strangers, many who would be strangers no more. The road was always rocky in the land where we traveled. The days were hot and dusty and the nights were cold. But whenever my heart would weaken or my feet stumble, my master was there to touch me, to lift me up, and renew my strength. I truly lived through the gentle, loving touch of my master's hand.

My master made many friends. But he also had enemies. Those who coveted power and riches and the favors of great men feared my master and sought to destroy him. But until he allowed it, evil men had no power over my master.

Soon, my master began asking other men, special men, to travel with us. They too had seen the light in my master's eyes and felt the power in his touch. One by one, he gathered them from the places where we walked and taught them about his Father. They brought very few possessions with them, because my master promised that he would provide all that they needed. I had always carried my master's few belongings and now I also carried things for these other men too. They treated me well, oftentimes sharing an apple or some other juicy morsel with me. I enjoyed their company and though I was no longer young and spry, I was still very strong. It was no burden for me to help them. They loved my master too, so we all shared a common bond. And this bond gave us strength.

Kindling a Dying Flame

"Careful now, Meshak, we've been together too long for me to lose you now." It was a cool, crisp morning when my master led me down a very steep hillside. I scrambled and stumbled and almost rolled to the bottom. The dust settled and we stood together at the bottom of the steep hill and looked around.

We came here alone, the two of us. There were people all around this deep, steep-sided valley. "Meshak, do you see the dark caves in the rocky walls of this valley?"

He pointed where he wanted me to look. "People live in those caves."

Many of the people came close as we walked through the small valley toward the dark openings on the other side.

There was a strange smell here, one which caused the flesh to creep on my neck. It made me feel afraid. I stopped and felt an overwhelming urge to run—run back up the slope, away from these people; away from this strange smell, from the blanketed whispers and shuffling steps most of the people made; away from the faces so

often covered with cloth; away from the hands and feet hidden beneath gauze wrappings. There was sickness and death here. I could feel it, thick like honey, cloying and sticky.

They came with their hands held out as though they wanted us to give them something. But we had brought nothing with us—no food, no clothes, no money. My master moved forward, so I put my head down and stared straight at his sandaled feet and nothing else. I followed closely and carefully in his wake, my legs quivering in fear with each step.

"Meshak, don't be afraid." My master turned and spoke softly so that only I could hear. "These people are lepers, Meshak, and have been cast out of their homes by people who fear their disease and their deformity."

I looked around at the huddled groups of murmuring people, many dressed in rags and gauze wrappings. I too was afraid of them.

"Meshak, these people need our love and acceptance even more than those whose bodies are whole. They did nothing to deserve this curse which has been placed upon them." Again he touched my head and looked into my eyes. It was as though he poured courage into my heart and mind. My quaking knees became still and I was no longer afraid.

My master turned once more to the crowds of people, a welcoming smile on his face and in his eyes.

As they came closer, he spoke softly to the people and touched many of them. He seemed to have no fear and everywhere he went, some of the sadness seemed to lift.

Though he brought them no gold or silver, I knew my master brought them something much more valuable. He touched them and they felt his love flow deep into their hearts. He treated them as real people, something no one had done in far too long. He spoke to them of his Father's love for them. He promised that they would be whole again—if not in this lifetime, surely in the next. Many of them found hope and strength in the words my master spoke. They all found comfort, strength, and renewal in the touch of my master's hand.

We left that place, but a part of it went away with us. My master did not seem to stand as straight as he had before. I think his soul was weighed down by their despair. I nuzzled his hand as it hung by his side, seeking to understand and share some of the pain I knew he was feeling.

My master stopped and sat on a large stone beside the dusty road we were following. He watched the people passing, looking carefully into their faces.

"Meshak, I am troubled because so many people who are whole on the outside are silently hiding their cankering disease deep inside where it festers and rots them from within."

I looked more carefully at the people hurrying past us. I began to see what my master was trying to teach me. Some of the people radiated their own light that seemed to shine from within. None were as strong as my master's light, but those people seemed brighter as they walked past us. Once I saw their brightness, it became obvious that others seemed to be walking in a dark shadow. It was

as though my eyes were open for the very first time. Even as these people walked side by side or passed each other along the road, they could not yet see the light and darkness that surrounded them.

"You see it now, don't you, my friend?" My master was smiling at me with pride. "You are looking with new eyes and can now see the people who have filled their inside lamps with oil." He looked back again at the passing travelers and the smile faded from his face.

"You can also see those who have not filled their inside lamps, whose lights are very dim. Some have even gone out."

I watched the people and felt chills tingling down my spine and making my heart beat very fast.

"This is why I'm here, Meshak. I have come to pour oil into their lamps and to light a fire within their souls," his voice was soft as he spoke, "if they'll let me."

He turned and looked into my eyes. With all the power in my heart, I told him that I too could envision a world where everyone walked in their own circle of light, how kind and loving people in that world would be. I poured out my love for him and let him know that I now understood the overwhelming task to which he had committed his life.

"Look there, my friend." He nodded his head at an old man coming toward us, his eyes staring straight at the ground, a frown on his lips and no light in his face. "Come, Meshak, let's see if we can brighten the day for this man. He looks like he could use a friend."

My master stepped into the center of the road and

watched the old man approach. I stood at his side.

"Grandfather," spoke my master. The old man looked up, the frown on his face even heavier than before as he glared into my master's face.

"The road is long, and hot, and dusty," my master spoke with gentle kindness in his voice.

"So! You have stopped me to tell me something I already know!" The old man looked back down at the ground and took a step forward. "Get out of my way! I'm already late and I don't have time to talk with fools!"

"I had a grandfather once." My master stepped aside to let the man pass, then turned and walked along beside him. "His bones ached and his feet hurt when he walked a long way. When I was a boy, I loved to take him for rides on my little burro." He patted my back and the old man glanced over at me.

"Hmmmmph!" grunted the old man.

"When my grandfather rode on Meshak here, his feet didn't hurt anymore and his bones didn't ache as much. Then he would tell me the most wonderful stories of when he was a young boy. I loved those days."

"Hmmmmph!" grunted the old man again.

We climbed one more hill, walking beside the old man, before my master finally convinced him to ride upon my back. Long before we reached the next city, the old man was smiling and recounting memories from his own childhood. My master laughed with him through the funny stories and cried with him through the sad ones.

When we left this grandfather in the city and went

our own way, the frown was no longer etched deeply into his mouth or his heart. A bit of light was shining from his eyes and I knew he had opened his lamp and let my master pour in some oil and light the wick. I stood there amazed as I watched a brighter, happier man wave at us as he stepped through a doorway and disappeared into a building.

I looked inquiringly up at my master.

"His light wasn't all the way out, Meshak, it was just buried beneath too many burdens. He needed someone to lift those burdens long enough for him to feel the warmth and see the light of his own lamp." He ruffled the hair on my forehead, then turned to go. "You helped me lift his burdens and fuel his light, my friend. Thank you."

Miracles

We waited in the cool shadow of a tall tree and watched the gathering crowd of followers come ever closer and spread out around us. The skirts of their robes formed a wall encircling us, so that I could no longer see the surrounding mountainside. Rich colors next to faded material, new sandals next to old ones, washed and sweet smelling bodies mingling with the sweaty and travel-stained people who had all come to hear my master's message. He stood before them, a gentle smile of love and understanding lighting his face.

Tall mountains rose behind my master as he climbed up on a rock so that all could see him. While I grazed at his feet, he turned to face the multitude. Massive swirling clouds of gray and black filled the sky above the mountains behind him. Silver light reflected across the hillside, deepening the green of the grass and brightening the colors of the wildflowers.

I reached down to nibble at the delicious grass as my master raised his hands for silence and the excited babble of voices ceased. Even as I searched out the newest,

sweetest shoots of grass to eat, the people who had followed my master sat down amongst the rocks and grass and flowers, eager to hear the words he would speak. The curtain of legs and robes disappeared and I could look out across the great gathering of curious people.

My master spoke and they listened. "Blessed are the poor in spirit, for theirs is the kingdom of heaven . . ."

In the distance, I saw many still coming to join the throng. There were the crippled and lame who used sticks to walk, limping and hobbling painfully behind the others, the blind led by those who could see, and the ever present lepers wrapped in their white robes and standing apart.

"Blessed are the meek, for they shall inherit the earth . . ."

I had never seen so many people gathered together in one place. Some of the people already glowed with their own special lights. But others had come in search of the oil that would fill their lamps and the spark to light a fire within their hearts.

"Let your light so shine before men that they may see your good deeds . . ."

For hours, sitting under the dark, ominous sky, they watched and drank in his words as my master spoke of a better place and a better world. He told them of a kingdom where people loved each other, cared for one another, and were happy—where no wars raged and no evil could exist.

Thunder crackled in the distance. He told them to love one another and to love their God. Giant drops of

rain fell from the boiling clouds. My master spoke of bap-
tism and of sacrifice, of masters and servants.

"Ask, and it shall be given you; seek, and ye shall find;
knock, and it shall be opened unto you: For every one
that asketh receiveth; and he that seeketh findeth; and to
him that knocketh it shall be opened . . ."

The rain ceased and they listened until the light
began to fail and evening approached. My master
touched many of the lame and they walked. He looked
into the eyes of the blind and they could see. He told the
lepers they were clean and their rotting flesh was made
whole again.

Looking across the vast sea of ardent faces, my master
ceased speaking for a moment. I could feel his empathy
for the people to whom he spoke, indeed for all the people of the world. I shared his love and delight for those
whose lights shone brightly. And I could sense his sadness and compassion for those who could not open their
lamps to accept the oil which he tried so hard to share.

He stood quietly for a time, his emotions warming the
air around him with a source far different from the sun.
Some felt his gift, so freely offered, but many did not. Soon
a murmur went through the crowd. The moment passed.
Then my master called to a young boy who had made his
way through the crowd to sit on the ground not far from
my master's feet. The boy came forward and brought with
him two baskets—one with five loaves of bread and the
other with two fishes in it.

The crowd hushed as my master stood before them.
Bowing his head, he blessed the bread and fish, then

divided them into pieces in the two baskets. Turning, he called me from where I waited behind him. I walked forward and stood before him, looking up into his face.

"Meshak, the green grass is sweet and you have eaten until your sides are bulging." He grinned at me and I waggled my ears back and forth in happy agreement. "But these people," he waved his hand, including all the people gathered on the hillside, "have had nothing to eat and they are hungry."

I looked at the people as they quietly watched my master, a few murmuring with curiosity. Then I looked back into his eyes.

"I would like you to carry these baskets among the people so that they might have food as well." I looked into the baskets and knew there was not enough food to feed everyone gathered on the mountainside. I gazed into his eyes again.

"Don't worry, my friend, there will be enough." It was a small favor my master asked of me and I eagerly waggled my ears to say 'yes'.

The crowd rose to their feet and though I feared the press of so many people, I walked carefully among them. Several of the men who also followed my master walked with me to control the crowd. Countless hands grasped eagerly, hungrily for the food which I carried. I feared many times that they would mob me and take all that I had. There was so little and they were very hungry. I saw their hands come away from the baskets full of bread and bits of fish. I wondered how could they be so selfish and take so much.

The farther I walked, the heavier my burden became until my legs grew weak and my breaths came in labored gasps. Still the hands pushed and pulled me, grabbing for even more food from my baskets. The men beside me saw me weaken and a quiet, strong man quickly lifted one of the baskets from my back. I felt the relief instantly. My load was not nearly as heavy now.

As the man walked in front of me, I saw that the basket he carried was full to overflowing with pieces of fish—and I did not understand. Again the basket I was carrying grew too heavy. The men leading and following me divided some of my load into other baskets which they gathered from amongst the crowd, and we continued on.

When at last all of the people had eaten their fill, I was very tired and I returned to stand behind my master. I hung my head between my front hooves, my labored breaths blowing hot air on the wild flowers at my feet. Curiously, I turned my head to watch as my master removed the last basket from my back. It was overflowing with pieces of bread, far more than had been in the basket when I first walked into the crowd.

The people also watched and an excited murmur spread throughout the assembled crowd. They spoke of a miracle, surely the greatest of the many they had seen this day. Their strength renewed, the crowd surged forward, the lame and sick desperate to reach my master, sure that he could heal them with just a touch. My master would have blessed many more, but the crowd became too excited, too irreverent, too dangerous.

As the sun slid below the edge of the earth, my master and I quietly slipped away, climbing higher into the mountain, into the darkness. From a secluded spot high on the mountain, we watched their confusion as word of my master's disappearance spread through the crowd.

"Thank you, Meshak." His voice sounded weary as he sat beside me and draped one arm across my back. "They will remember the food you brought for their bodies," he paused for a moment, continuing to look across the distance at the people who had eaten the bread and fish. They were meandering back toward the road and their homes now. "But will they remember the food I brought for their souls?"

How I wished I could speak and tell him with words how wonderful I thought he was and how I was sure the people would remember many of his teachings. I turned my head to look at him and nickered softly.

"Yes, Meshak, I understand, and I appreciate your faith in me." His fingers scratched between my ears, then he stood up. "Come, let's get you a drink of water and a few oats to go with all that grass." I let out a joyful hee-haw as he opened the pack bags.

My master poured water for me, but did not take any for himself. As I munched on sweet oats, my master knelt beside a large, flat rock, and raised his eyes to a hole in the dark clouds where the black sky glittered with sparkling stars. His shoulders seemed bowed, weighed down with some enormous burden.

I went to stand beside him and gently touched his shoulder with my nose. He turned and looked into my

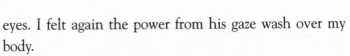

eyes. I felt again the power from his gaze wash over my body.

"My oil is running low, Meshak. I need to fill my lamp again and there is only one who can help me do that."

I had always wondered why he looked to the stars so often and in my quiet way, I asked him, "Who?"

"He is my Father who lives among the stars. He is the one, great Father of all. The creator of the universe, of me—and of you, Meshak." My master spoke simply so that I could understand.

I looked up through the dwindling hole in the clouds, but all I saw were stars.

"Trust me, Meshak. He's there." He spoke quietly, but with immense power. Though I didn't understand completely, I believed in my master and I trusted his words.

"Go to sleep, my friend. Morning will come and we have far to go. You will need all your energy, so get some rest now."

I searched for a soft spot beneath a tree, then bent my knees and dropped to the ground. As I watched him before my eyelids closed, it seemed to me that a gentle halo of light filled his face and the air all around him. I looked for the terra cotta lamp and saw it laying partially in and partially out of the pack which I carried each day. But it was not lit tonight.

As I continued to watch, it seemed that the weight lifted from his shoulders just a bit. I closed my eyes, curled my legs closer to my body and laid my head back down on the ground, trying once again to go to sleep. My last thoughts before I drifted into dreamland were that

my master had learned his lesson well. He had never again forgotten to fill his lamps with oil—neither the one outside, nor the one inside.

My Master's Touch

My nose, once velvet white with a black ring around it, was almost completely gray now. My tail still had a few black strands in it, but I noticed that it had become shorter and stiffer than when I was young. My hooves were cracked and splayed because of the many years I had walked over the hard, rocky ground. The middle of my back had developed a deep sway in it that wouldn't rise up, no matter how hard I tried. It was getting more and more difficult each morning to push myself up onto all four feet. My heart was always willing, but often my stiff, old body would not respond to my commands. On the mornings when it was hardest to get my creaking bones to cooperate, my master would touch me with his gentle hands and the pains would fade away for a time. I followed him as always, but he no longer rode on my back as he had as a boy and later as a young man. Instead, he walked by my side or led the way for me to follow.

Once more he asked if I would rather rest my last days

in a warm bed of straw rather than follow him through the mountains and villages of men. And, as always before, he looked deep into my soul for the answer. I would follow him as long as I had breath and could hobble behind him.

Life for my master was not easy either. Many were the wicked men who sought to harm my master for the good things he taught. You see, it is hard to hold mastery over a man who sees beyond the slavery of this world. Many were the times when wicked men, with no light in their souls, sought to put my master in prison or even kill him. They could not see that guardian angels protected my master for the time he was to teach his message.

I watched my master heal the sick, give sight to the blind, help the lame to walk again, and even bring the dead back to life.

But our most enjoyable times were those we spent with the children. Their laughter and enthusiasm helped him relax and forget about the days ahead.

"While they are young, Meshak," said my master as he placed a small boy on my back, "children all have a light that shines from within."

I walked through tall grass beneath the shady trees and he walked alongside to make sure the boy did not slip off. "It is only as they grow older that many of their lights are put out by others around them." We wove in and out among the tree trunks, walking in a large circle as other children cheered and eagerly waited for their turns.

I stopped and waited in the center of the excited

group of children as my master helped the boy down and lifted a bright-eyed little girl up onto my back and showed her how to hold onto my mane. Then he continued, "Others just let their lamps run dry. They spend the rest of their lives searching for a way to relight their lamps." A sigh escaped his lips. "But so many never open their lamps to let the oil in."

We spent some wonderful, unforgettable days at rivers. He laughed as I stood in the water, letting the little children crawl onto my back and fall off into the water. The children doused him with water until soon he was in the river, frolicking right along with them. In the midst of the laughter and fun, my master always found opportunities to teach them to love one another and share each other's burdens. Those days reminded us both of the carefree times when we were young and playing in the streets and hills of his home.

My master's reputation had spread throughout the land and every day groups of people would seek him out to ask for a blessing or to listen to the principles which he taught.

I began to wonder how much longer my old body would be able to rise up in the morning and follow him. Then one morning, I struggled hard just to get to my knees. But no matter how hard I tried, I could not get up onto my feet. I was too old. My legs had finally given up. Sharp pains stabbed through my back and neck and my eyes had become blurry so that I no longer saw the world clearly. I stopped struggling for a moment. I needed to rest.

"Meshak, my old friend." I perked up my ears as I

heard my master's voice above me. I tried, but I could not raise my head high enough to look into his eyes.

"Here, let me kneel beside you." He took my head into his hands once more, but this time he raised his eyes to the sky above. As I listened intently, he asked for a special blessing from his Father for my sake. He spoke of our years together and asked that I be granted the strength I would need to continue as his companion. As I listened in awe to the words he spoke, I felt power and strength return to my body. The pains faded away and my heart and soul were renewed once again.

"There, is that better?" he asked as he looked into my eyes once more.

I waggled my ears and nickered in reply. Then, with his support, I struggled to my feet and he held me until my legs ceased shaking and I had the strength to stand alone.

"Our lives on this earth do not go on forever, my friend." He stroked my ears as he looked around at the special group of men who traveled with us. Some were sitting, some standing, but all were watching his every action and listening to each of his words. Some were amazed that he should care for one as humble as I.

"Though I would rather sit by the riverbank with you and watch the children play, or lay beneath a shady tree and watch the clouds chase across the sky . . ." He paused and spoke very slowly while he looked at something only he could see, somewhere far away in the distance. "I know . . . that it is now time for me to go to Jerusalem."

The Last Road

The very way he said those words turned my heart cold. We had been to Jerusalem before, but the tone in his voice told me he knew this time would be different.

As we reached the outskirts of Jerusalem and gazed at the massive wall protecting the city, the spring sunshine was bright and the air fresh. My master stopped outside the city gates and told several of his followers where to find a special young white burro for him to ride into the great city.

When they had departed in search of the white donkey, my master took my head between his loving hands once more. That familiar tingling feeling of power and love coursed through my whole body. "Meshak, my faithful friend, long ago a great man told his people of this day—the day that I would ride into Jerusalem on a white donkey. He made the prophecy. And I have come to fulfill it." My master could see that I did not understand—did not want to understand.

"Can't you ride me? I can be strong enough for this one day? Why not me?" He could read my thoughts in my pleading eyes and drooping ears.

"Not this time, Meshak. Wait here, my faithful one, and I will come back for you." He turned and walked to where his men had returned and were waiting with the white donkey. I held my head high, trying to act brave, but deep inside it broke my heart. Tears filled my eyes as I watched him ride away on the young, beautiful little animal.

It was a strong, fine colt and well able to carry my master. When he rode down the road to Jerusalem, the crowds opened before my master and closed behind him. I couldn't wait here alone. I had to follow. So I hurried after him, as fast as I could force myself to go for I could not bear to be left behind.

Cheering people threw palm leaves before the hooves of the little donkey as a welcome to my master. I lost him in the great crowds gathered to see him and listen to his words. Many pressed forward to touch just the hem of his garment that they might be healed. My tottering old legs could not keep up with the younger donkey and soon there were many people between my master and me. It wasn't long before I could no longer hear his voice nor see the little white donkey. Sandaled feet and colorful robes blocked my view.

My hooves hurt and my breath came in painful gasps. I stumbled on and on, but finally I could go no further. I stopped. Trembling, I stood there, my heart breaking with loneliness, sides heaving, legs shaking, my nose

almost touching the ground. A great rushing sound filled my head and the world started to spin around me. I stumbled, afraid I would fall.

"Out of my way, you old bag of bones!" A dark-faced man shoved me aside. The crowds surged past me, shoving and bumping me, cursing me for being in their way, jeering at my broken-down body. I could feel the hot tears welling in my eyes, tumbling in streams down my face and dripping into the dry dust of that hot street. Soon they all passed and I was alone. The crowds had gone on ahead, following my master, going where I wanted to go.

The street was quiet. Noisy flies buzzed past, some stopping to bite me. I was too weak to even switch them with my tail. It took every bit of strength I could summon to remain standing. I stood there a long time, not daring to move, but promising myself—one more breath. Just one more, then I'll follow him.

I did not hear him come this time. He was just there. I felt his hands on my neck. Felt them gently stroke my fuzzy mane and travel down to my gray and grizzled head. One hand held my chin up while the other stroked my neck and scratched gently behind my big floppy ears. I gazed at him through my tears and I saw again his gentle smile. I felt the warmth and strength from the healing touch of his hands flow through my old, tired body and I was restored once more. My heart calmed, the tremors in my legs ceased and I smiled at him with my eyes and wobbled my ears back and forth, for that was the only way I had of speaking to him and telling my master how much I loved him.

"You didn't think I would leave behind my oldest friend, did you, Meshak?" He pulled my face close to his and in a very soft whisper said, "We have always been together and I will not leave you. We won't travel much longer, the end of our journey is near—you must go on but just a short time more." He looked deep within my soul and asked for the last time, "Can you follow me to the very end, my most faithful friend?"

He heard my silent answer. Then he smiled and stood once more before me. I looked down at his feet, scarred from our many travels, dust stained, protected from the rocks by the same old leather sandals—and I was content once again.

Together we walked slowly through the streets to a small turning where two small stalls were hidden beneath a stairway. There stood the young, white colt, greedily eating the hay in his manger. My master took me into the other stall and fluffed a bed of clean straw and filled my manger with sweet hay. He placed cool water in the trough and bid me lay down and wait for him once more.

I drank my fill, then ate a bit of the hay. Soon I lay down on the soft bed and listened for my master's voice from the room above. I heard him bless bread and wine and speak of the time he would be here no more. His words brought tears to my eyes. Then I heard the sounds of washing and from their words, knew that my master was washing the feet of those men who followed him most closely and tried hardest to follow his teachings. He was trying to teach them that the greatest among them

would be the one who served the others.

A short time later, one man, alone, crept quietly down the steps and with many guilty backward glances, disappeared into the darkness. My heart froze, touched with an icy fear I did not understand, a fear for my master like none I'd ever felt before. I knew this man. My master and I had traveled with him for many months now. But tonight he had no light in his face and I knew that he had allowed his lamp to run dry.

Lonely Sacrifice

*I*t was late and the streets were empty when the other men came down the stairs once more. My master was among them. Gritting my teeth and using every bit of strength I could muster, I struggled to my feet and followed them through the dark streets and out of the city to a hill covered with olive trees. The sweet smell reminded me of those nights, oh so many years ago, when we two had walked in the darkness to gather wood for my master's mother. I wondered what my master would gather here on this night. He carried no lamp to light the path before him, but his feet did not falter. He walked on as though he knew this path very well.

The men who had come there with my master sat themselves down on the ground and spoke in whispers for a short time as my master continued on up the hill a short distance further. I hobbled past them, following after him, not wanting my master to be alone out there in the dark, nor wanting to be alone myself.

When he stopped and knelt, I bent my old knees and dropped to the ground in the deep shadows of an old, gnarled olive tree where I could watch my master and hear his voice. His face turned toward the bright star shining high in the heavens. The words he spoke were full of promise and sorrow, pleading and love. Again, I saw that familiar, beautiful aura of light radiate from his face. His words frightened me and I did not understand many of the things that happened then, nor can I even begin to explain them.

I just know that I desperately wanted to go to him, to comfort him in some way. But I felt frozen to the ground. It was as though heavy chains bound me in place. I could not move, could barely breathe, imprisoned by some unseen hand. The light from my master's face seemed to fade, as though the oil in his lamp was running low and the flame about to go out.

"Father, please, don't leave me alone! I need thy help!" My master's anguished voice rose in desperate petition to that Father upon whose business he had come.

He cried out in pain and despair. I struggled frantically to get up, but I couldn't move. I could only watch and listen.

Halting and strained, his soft voice cried, "Father, I suffer this . . . willingly . . . because of the love I have for all of my brothers and sisters." The words he spoke next were too beautiful to repeat, too heartfelt to share. Just as I thought my heart would surely break, the light in his face grew brighter and his body relaxed. Gradually, I felt

Lynda M. Nelson

that awful, strangling force release me. It was over. My master's lamp seemed once more to be filled to the brim, for the light shining from his face was far brighter than I had ever seen it before.

Time passed till, shaking and unsteady, my master rose and turned to me. No words were spoken, but I felt him say in his heart, "Thank you, my old friend, for staying with me while the others slept."

I turned my eyes to the men who had followed him. Truly, they were all asleep. Though these few, faithful men all loved him, my master had struggled through this darkest hour of his eternity alone—almost.

The night was cold, the ground damp. My legs struggled to push my body upright and I tottered after him once more. I was too slow and fell farther and farther behind. I was frightened by a sudden, terrible yelling and arguing ahead of me. When I finally reached the bottom of the hill, I saw wicked men had seized my master and were dragging him away.

I hobbled after them as fast as I could, but they grew steadily further and further away from me. Finally, I turned a corner in the great city and could no longer see or hear them.

He was gone. My master had been taken from me. I had no idea where to go to find him. Then out of the darkness came one of the men who had also followed my master. Never failing in his love for me, my master had sent this one to find me and be sure that I was safe. Sadly,

74

my footsteps faltering and slow, I followed this friend of my master's to a small stable close to a noisy inn.

The Hill

Days passed and I heard only scattered bits of news about my master from those who came in and out of the stable. Then one evening, just before dark, the gate opened and there before me was my master's gentle mother. Somewhere in time, she had grown older as well. But the silver in her beautiful hair only made her more lovely in my eyes. She sat down beside me in the clean, dry straw and stayed beside me for many hours, stroking my ears, and speaking to me of her love for her son. She hugged me and her tears mingled with mine as we relived our memories together and sent our love out through the dark night to wherever my master was, hoping he would feel our love for him, know that we waited for him, that we prayed for him.

The next morning, I heard a great commotion outside. For the first time in days, I struggled to my knees. My heart beat faster while I strained to hear the shouted words. People in the streets were speaking my master's name.

Suddenly, the gate burst open and my master's mother stood before me. "Meshak," she called, "come with me. I have heard where they have taken my son."

I struggled to my feet, using every bit of determination and strength in my body. "Good boy, Meshak. I knew you could do it." Her kind words gave me added strength and together we followed the crowds that were gathering—eager to find her son, my master, once more; eager for one more sight of his kind face, one more touch of his hand.

When at last we found him, our eyes filled with tears and our hearts broke within us. My master had a crown of thorns piercing the skin of his head and he was dragging a giant cross of wood on the road to Golgotha.

I dragged my shaking body up the hill, following his sobbing mother, as he drug that wicked cross. My heart lightened a bit when another man helped him. But as the evil men drove nails into his hands and feet and raised him bleeding and in pain up for the crowds to jeer, I trembled and fell to the ground, surely for the last time.

I looked up at him, wishing I could take away his pain, wishing his path could have taken a different turn than the one that had led to this awful place.

My master's mother stood beneath her son and touched him gently, one last time in this life. She was beautiful as she had always been and her tears only made her more lovely. If she had the strength to withstand this pain, then I too could not give up, could not let her stand there alone. I struggled once more to my feet and limped slowly up to her side.

One Roman soldier stood there laughing at the torment and pain he had caused. Suddenly, the rage and fury in my heart surged through my muscles. I felt powered with enormous energy. I couldn't just stand there any longer.

I whirled around to charge into that laughing Roman soldier and knock him sprawling across the rocky ground.

"Meshak, stop! You'll only get yourself killed!" My master's mother threw her arms around my neck and drug me backwards, away from the soldiers. "Meshak . . . my son gives his life willingly . . . He is making this sacrifice because his Father in Heaven asked him to do it . . . for all the people of this earth." Her tear-filled eyes looked into mine and I felt the great love she had for my master.

"This sacrifice was *his* choice, Meshak!" Her sorrow wrenched at my aching heart. "We must have faith in what he is doing. Even now, we must not lose our hope for the future that he has promised us . . . if we will follow his teachings. He taught that we must have love even for our enemies." A sob escaped her lips. "No matter . . . how hard . . . it may be."

She raised her eyes upward. "Oh, my son, my son . . ."

Suddenly, my master's voice echoed across the hillside, and everyone looked up to his pain-wracked face. "Father . . . forgive them . . . for they know not what they do!"

As I stared upwards, my master looked down into my eyes. His silent message burned across the distance, through my eyes, and into my mind. "There is already

too much pain and anger in this world, Meshak. I came to teach love and kindness. Follow in my footsteps once more, my friend—do as I would do!"

The anger drained away and I was left with only the warmth and strength his gaze always brought to me.

For hours, those who loved him most sat huddled beneath his feet in sadness and misery. We were trying earnestly to share his suffering, and easing it by having him know we were there. But the one who could truly help seemed to be far away. Some said that the Heavenly Father whom my master served went into the farthest corner of his great universe and cried while his son suffered on the cross.

His pain and suffering ripped into our hearts as my master cried out in his anguish, "My God . . . my God . . . why hast thou forsaken me?"

My heart pleaded with different words, "Please, master, go on to that better place you have told me about so many times. Leave this world of pain and misery—go where there is only love and kindness, where all the lights shine brightly."

Once more I heard my master's pain-filled voice and his rasping words filled my heart with relief as he cried out, "Father . . . into *thy* hands . . . I commend my spirit."

We looked upward once more and saw that his light had gone out completely. His body still hung from the cross, but his spirit had flown. He suffered no longer.

Come Follow Me

His mother and I cried together, walking slowly home, leaning on each other for support, surrounded by those who mourned with us.

My master's mother gave me a final hug and told me to rest. As I lowered my weary body down onto the soft bed she had prepared for me, she laid an old, faded blanket across my back to keep out the chill night air. It was the same blanket I had carried for my master through the years of our travels. Then, taking the little terra cotta lamp out of my pack bag, she lit the wick and placed the lamp on a high shelf so that it's golden light fell around me. One final pat on my head and she quietly went out, slowly closing the stable gate behind her.

I touched my nose to the soft, well-worn blanket and tears seeped through my tightly closed eyelids as I inhaled his familiar scent.

Tears continued to trickle down my shaggy face, dripping from my gray muzzle to the stable floor. Tears—not because he was gone—but that I was left to go on alone.

He had been my strength and my reason for living.

You see, my mother had carried his mother on that day so very long ago when she and her young husband journeyed to Bethlehem. The night my mother gave birth to me, my master was also born. I was there, blinking in the light of this new world and stumbling to my wobbly legs as the light of a dazzling new star gleamed through the window of the stable and my master's first cry was heard.

I was there when the shepherds came. Their eyes were full of wonder and their hearts full of the words and songs the glorious angels had shared with them. I shared their wonder as I too heard shimmering angels sing to this child. Then I toddled over to the beautiful lady who held him so lovingly and reached my little nose curiously up to see why this tiny bundle caused so much fuss.

It was then that his precious little hand reached out of that special blanket and I felt my master's touch for the first time. I was changed forever. I was as new to this world as he was, yet somehow I knew that I would follow him all my life. We came into this world together and we would go out of it together.

But now here I was, in a stable once more. But this time I was all alone—no bright star, no angels singing, no wise men with chests of frankincense, myrrh and gold. My master had left me and I was lost without him. My heart felt broken, all shriveled up inside my chest. The pain was intense and the tears falling from my eyes made it even harder to breathe.

Tears clouded my eyes as I raised them to look once

more at the familiar little lamp with its golden light. The flame wavered and seemed to be encircled by a colorful halo. I thought again of that night so long ago when the oil had run out of the little lamp, leaving us alone in the darkness. I thought again of the faith my master had shown in me as he asked me to carry him out of the darkness and into the light once again. And I remembered also the warmth and love, courage and strength that I received each time I felt my master's touch. I let out a very quiet nicker, then closed my eyes and lowered my chin until it rested on the edge of the blanket, finally too sad and too tired to hold my head up any longer.

I did not see the light that slowly filled the small stable. I did not hear him come. But I knew his hand when I felt it touch my head. I did not open my eyes as I felt gentle fingers raise my chin and stroke my floppy ears and fuzzy mane. I was afraid it was a dream. But when I heard his sweet voice, I opened my eyes, blurred with tears. "You didn't think I would leave you alone, did you, my faithful little friend?"

The room was full of light and I could barely look at him, for my master glowed with a radiance far brighter than the sun at noontime. But I knew his voice and I knew the touch of my master's hand.

He spoke once more and said, "Come, my faithful Meshak. Come follow me." He was my master and my shepherd and I would follow where ever he led. When I stood this time, there was no pain in my body. It was as though I was young again.

And I followed him.

Now and Forever

*M*ary came into the stable early in the morning to feed the little burro that had been her son's friend through his life and found the little body cold and lifeless beneath the faded blanket. She reached down to touch the soft muzzle, totally silver now.

"I know you are with him and how I wish I could be with you both." The tears that were so fresh yesterday ran freely down her face. "Follow and watch after him till I see you both again."

Mary stood and reached up to lift the small lamp down from the shelf above the stall. With a gentle puff of air, she blew out the golden flame. She turned to leave, but paused a moment. Bending, she laid the still-smoking lamp beside the small burro, then stood and went out of the stable, shutting the gate softly behind her.

The End